T0147178

GOD'S POWER
UNLEASHED

KEYS TO REVIVAL

CARLA MORRIS

WESTBOW
PRESS®
A DIVISION OF THOMAS NELSON
& ZONDERVAN

WestBow Press books may be ordered through booksellers or by contacting:

WestBow Press
A Division of Thomas Nelson & Zondervan
1663 Liberty Drive
Bloomington, IN 47403
www.westbowpress.com
844-714-3454

ISBN: 978-1-6642-4978-3 (sc)
ISBN: 978-1-6642-4979-0 (hc)
ISBN: 978-1-6642-4977-6 (e)

Library of Congress Control Number: 2021923185

Print information available on the last page.

WestBow Press rev. date: 7/26/2022

To my mother, Lois Wyche,
who raised me in a church where I was
able to experience God's Spirit and
the gifts He so freely gives us. And to
my late husband, Michael Morris,
who encouraged me throughout our
marriage to follow God's calling.

REVIVAL IN THE NEW ERA

The Lord has given many prophetic words about a massive revival during this next season. He is going to reap a harvest before His return. For this to happen, the church needs to move in the gifts at a deeper level. We need to step out in faith and prophesy, heal the sick, raise the dead, deliver those who are possessed. Revival will only come when we have received the baptism of the Holy Spirit and have stirred up the gifts God has given us. It is our responsibility. God is not going to force Himself on us. We are to seek Him and respond to His prompting. Miracles are still available to us today. They are God's desire for this planet. Christians can no longer sit by passively and hope for a good result. There is a battle raging in our society for the souls of every person. The media presents us with false gods and idols every day. Satan is the ultimate counterfeiter. He loves to take that which is of God and make it seem commonplace by presenting a counterfeit. As Christians, we have the real deal. We have the Holy Spirit working in us. God has given gifts to the church today. As we will see in the upcoming chapters, they have many purposes. However, the most crucial goal of the gifts is to bring others to Christ. God is bringing revival during this next era, like none we have seen in the past. The church needs to prepare.

GIFTS OF THE SPIRIT

Now concerning spiritual gifts, brethren, I do not want you to be ignorant: You know that you were Gentiles, carried away to these dumb idols; however you were led. Therefore I make known to you that no one speaking by the Spirit of God calls Jesus accursed, and no one can say that Jesus is Lord except by the Holy Spirit. There are diversities of gifts, but the same Spirit. There are differences of ministries, but the same Lord. And there are diversities of activities, but it is the same God who works all in all. But the manifestation of the Spirit is given to each one for the profit of all: for to one is given the word of wisdom through the Spirit, to another the word of knowledge through the same Spirit, to another faith by the same Spirit, to another gifts of healing by the same Spirit, to another the working of miracles, to another prophecy, to another discerning of spirits, to another different kinds of tongues, to another the interpretation of tongues. But one and the same Spirit works all these things, distributing to each one individually as He wills.

—1 Corinthians 12:1–11 (NKJV)

GOD WANTS TO reveal Himself to us. He wants us to know who He is and be part of His kingdom on earth. God uses the gifts of the Holy Spirit to show us His plans not only for our own lives but also for the lives of those around us. He opens our eyes to the spirit world and allows us to be part of something much larger than ourselves. As we study the gifts of the Holy Spirit, we will have the opportunity to view the blueprint God has for His church.

The apostle Paul wrote these scriptures to the church in Corinth. It was a young church that had been in existence for about three years at that time. It was located in present-day Greece but was under the rule of the Roman Empire. Corinth was a polytheistic society. The Corinthians believed there were many different gods, and the worship of idols was commonplace. Statues honoring these gods lined the streets.

Paul wanted the church to understand that all of the gifts came from God in heaven. He did not want their past beliefs to creep back in and credit each gift to a pagan god. Paul repeatedly uses the phrase "same spirit." He emphasizes that each gift comes from the Holy Spirit and not from a pagan god of their past.

There are nine spiritual gifts listed in this passage:

- word of wisdom
- word of knowledge
- faith
- gifts of healing
- working of miracles
- prophecy
- discerning of spirits
- different kinds of tongues
- interpretation of tongues

First Corinthians 14:1 states we are to desire spiritual gifts. When we accept Christ as our savior, we have access to all of God's bountiful gifts. In Acts 8:15–17, the Holy Spirit filled the new believers when Philip laid hands on them and prayed for them. The various gifts of the Spirit are ours to access through our faith in Jesus. Once we receive the Holy Spirit, we are to fan into flames the gifts of God. It is our responsibility to apply faith to those gifts and begin using them.

> For this reason, I remind you to fan into flame the
> gift of God, which is in you through the laying on of
> my hands. (2 Timothy 1:6)

In Matthew 25:14–28, Jesus told a parable. A master was leaving on a journey, and he gave some of his servants some money to invest. Those who invested wisely were given more upon his return. However, the master took back the money from the one who did not use the gift wisely. God gives us gifts, but it is our responsibility to apply faith to those gifts and use them as God instructs. As our faith grows, so does our ability to touch others for Christ through the miraculous power of God.

God gave us the gifts of the Spirit for two reasons: the first is to bring non-Christians into a relationship with Christ. During Jesus's ministry on earth, a revival would often follow a word of knowledge or miraculous healing. Crowds would gather to see what was happening, and Jesus would teach them about God in heaven. Remember that these were not faithless people. However, they worshiped many different gods. Jesus used these opportunities to show those who gathered the truth and direct them to the one and only true God.

The apostles performed many signs and wonders among the people. And all the believers used to meet together in Solomon's Colonnade. No one else dared join them, even though they were highly regarded by the people. Nevertheless, more and more men and women believed in the Lord and were added to their number. As a result, people brought the sick into the streets and laid them on beds and mats so that at least Peter's shadow might fall on some of them as he passed by. Crowds gathered also from the towns around Jerusalem, bringing their sick and those tormented by impure spirits, and all of them were healed. (Acts 5:12–16)

In the book of Acts, revival followed when the Christian church moved in the gifts of the spirit. In Acts 2, God's spirit filled the disciples and their families. That day, more than three thousand people were saved. If we are going to have revival take place in the church today, we must move in spiritual gifts. They are the key to revival.

During the twentieth century, there were two major revivals that began in California. The first was the Azusa Street Revival. It started with a minister who came to Los Angeles and began teaching on the gifts of the spirit. As people began to move in the gifts of the spirit, many were saved. This revival touched the lives of hundreds of thousands of people throughout the world.

The second revival began in San Francisco. It was known as the Jesus movement. It also began with Christians using the gifts of the spirit to touch those around them. As people began to see the power of God in action, they turned their lives over to Him. Many of the churches we worship in today came out of the Jesus movement and the revival that took place.

The second purpose of the gifts is to strengthen, encourage, and comfort those who already believe in Jesus as their savior (1 Corinthians 14:3). As believers in Jesus Christ, we are in a battle. This battle is against demonic forces that want to discourage us and lead us away from the truth. As believers, we need one another. We need to use the gifts to help one another stand against the attacks of the enemy. Ephesians 6:17 says the spirit is our sword. We cannot go through life in isolation. We need to use the gifts we have to help one another.

> For our struggle is not against flesh and blood, but against the rulers, against the authorities, against the powers of this dark world and against the spiritual forces of evil in the heavenly realms. (Ephesians 6:12)

In the chapters that follow, we will explore each gift individually and learn how they work to bring revival and growth in the church.

GIFTS OF THE SPIRIT STUDY PAGES

Read Acts 1. What were the disciples doing prior to being filled with the Holy Spirit?

_____

_____

According to 2 Chronicles 8:12–13, what were the three annual festivals celebrated by the Israelites?

_____

_____

_____

Which of these three festivals were the people celebrating in Acts 1–2?

_____

_____

Read Exodus 34:22–27. The Celebration of Weeks was part of a covenant God made with Israel. Write down everything God promised to do as His part of the covenant.

_____

_____

_____

_____

What does it mean to you to have your territories enlarged?

_____

_____

In Luke 24:49, Jesus told the disciples He would clothe them in
_____ from on _____.

Read Mark 16:15–18. What signs does Jesus say will accompany
believers?

_____

_____

After the disciples received the Holy Spirit in Acts 2, Peter stood up
and addressed the crowd. Read Acts 2:14–41. Who did Peter say this
promise was for (verse 39)?

_____

_____

Peter quotes Joel 2:28–32. To whom will God pour out His spirit?

_____

_____

In Acts 2:22, Peter states that God accredited Jesus by
_____. _____.
and _____.

As we continue to study each gift individually, ask God to open your heart and mind to receive all that He has for you. Use the space below to write a commitment to God to open yourself up to fresh revelations.

_____

_____

_____

_____

_____

FAITH

Now faith is confidence in what we hope for and assurance about what we do not see.

—Hebrews 11:1

IN ORDER TO effectively use any of the gifts of the spirit, we must have faith in God—true conviction that God wants to speak to us, heal us, and show Himself to us through the miraculous. When we doubt God's ability or desire to meet us, we become immobilized and ineffective. When we move in faith, anything is possible through God (Matthew 17:20).

There are two keywords in Hebrews 11:1—*confidence* and *assurance*. Both are the same word in Greek, *hupostasis*. It means "the substance that allows us to stand under, endure, or undertake anything. A title deed as giving a guarantee" (*Vine's Expository Dictionary of New Testament Words*). The faith we have in God regulates our thoughts and actions. The gift of faith is an increased measure of faith that allows us to believe in the impossible.

With the gift of faith, we believe God will be there as we stand against the storms. We trust God will bring us through, no matter what we face. When we have this level of faith, the circumstances do not dictate what we believe. We can move forward, knowing that we have heard from God. He is our provider, protector, and healer.

In Hebrews chapter 11, Paul lists many of the Old Testament figures who possessed the gift of faith:

- Abel brought an offering to God. (Genesis 4)
- Enoch ascended to heaven without dying. (Genesis 5:24)
- Noah built an ark. (Genesis 6–9)
- Abraham moved his family to the Promised Land. (Genesis 12–17)
- Sarah gave birth to a child in her old age. (Genesis 17)
- Abraham offered Isaac as a sacrifice to God. (Genesis 22)
- Isaac blessed Jacob and Esau. (Genesis 27)
- Jacob blessed Joseph's children. (Genesis 48)
- Joseph prophesied about the Exodus from Egypt. (Genesis 48:21)
- Moses's parents hid him for three months and then put him in the river. (Exodus 2)
- Moses gave up his identity as the son of the Pharaoh's daughter. (Exodus 2)
- Israel passed through the Red Sea. (Exodus 14)
- The walls of Jericho fell. (Joshua 6)
- Rahab protected the Israeli spies. (Joshua 2)

After listing all of these, Paul wrote that there are many more people he did not have time to include. God spoke to each of these people. He gave them a level of faith that allowed them to continue to believe despite their circumstances.

When we have the gift of faith, we believe God will fulfill His word. God told Noah to build an ark. Noah most likely lived in the region of Mesopotamia, present-day Iraq. The people around Noah made fun of him. Building a massive ship seemed like a ridiculous use of time and money. The ark was not a small boat that could navigate the local rivers. It was huge. Noah continued to do what God told him to do despite the criticism. He had a level of faith that propelled him to complete the task he had begun. God saved Noah and his family when the rains flooded the earth (Genesis 6–9).

In the New Testament, we read of disciples who possessed the gift of faith. They were up against considerable opposition. Christianity was a new concept, and the disciples were opposing the norms of the time. The Jews had been teaching about the Messiah for thousands of years, but many rejected the idea that Jesus was the Messiah. Without faith, the disciples would not have been able to spread the Gospel and change the world.

Saul was an unbeliever until he had a life-changing encounter with God on the road to Damascus. That experience with God changed his life. It gave him a level of faith that resulted in many of the New Testament books. He was willing to go to prison and die for what he believed because his faith was unshakeable.

In Ephesians 6:16, Paul tells us that faith "extinguishes all the flaming arrows of the evil one." Faith is our counterattack as the devil tries to derail us with doubt and fear. When we have the gift of faith, the enemy is unable to get a foothold in our lives.

In Joshua 6, Joshua and his army were ready to attack the city of Jericho. A large wall surrounded the city, and the gates were securely barred. God spoke to Joshua and told him to circle the city blowing trumpets one time each day for six days. God gave Joshua very specific instructions. The army was to march around the city of Jericho once each day for six days. Seven priests blew trumpets as they circled the city. The army was to remain silent during these six days. They were not to attack or yell a battle cry. On the seventh day, the army circled the city seven times. On the seventh trip around the city, the army yelled a battle cry as the Lord had instructed Joshua. The walls of the city fell, and Joshua's army ceased the city. Joshua's faith and obedience allowed him to defeat his enemies (Joshua 6:1–27).

I love the quote "Ships do not sink because of the water around them; ships sink because of the water that gets in them" (author unknown). Faith allows us to keep water from getting in our ships. It propels us to believe God for the impossible. The gift of faith is a testimony to unbelievers and allows them to see we are different because of the God who lives in us.

Faith allows …

- us to be confident (Hebrews 1:1)
- our belief in God to not be shaken (Acts 2:25)
- us to believe God's promises in spite of our circumstances (Hebrews 11)

- us to conquer our enemies (Hebrews 11:33, Ephesians 6:16)
- us to be healed (Luke 8:48, 18:42)
- us to be successful (2 Chronicles 20:20)
- us to move mountains (Matthew 17:20)
- our sins to be forgiven (Mark 2:5, Luke 7:50)
- us to prophesy (Romans 12:6)
- us to be blessed (Galatians 3:9)
- us to approach God with freedom and confidence (Ephesians 3:12)

FAITH STUDY PAGES

Read Genesis 15:1–6.

What is credited as righteousness?

_____

_____

Read 1 Corinthians 2.

What produces faith (verse 5)?

_____

_____

How does having the Holy Spirit help us to have faith? (verses 11–12)

_____

_____

Look at each person listed in Hebrews 11. What were they able to do because of their faith in God?

_____

_____

_____

_____

In Mark 16:15–20, who does Jesus say will cast out demons, speak and tongues, pick up snakes and drink poison safely, and heal the sick?

_____

_____

Read Luke 24:46–49 and Acts 1:4–6.

Jesus tells the disciples to wait in the city for the Holy Spirit. What does He say they will be clothed with when they receive the Holy Spirit?

_____

_____

Read James 2:14–25.

What needs to accompany faith for it to be fruitful?

_____

_____

How do faith and action work together? What happens to faith without action?

_____

_____

Read Ephesians 6:16. How does faith shield us?
What does faith do to our enemies?

_____

_____

What are some ways you can stir up the gift of faith in your own life? How will that help you to move in the other gifts of the spirit?

_____

_____

PROPHESY

Follow the way of love and eagerly desire gifts of the Spirit, especially prophecy.

—1 Corinthians 14:1

HEARING GOD'S VOICE is essential to our relationship with Him. In John 10:1–5, Jesus tells the parable of the good shepherd. In this parable, we read that a shepherd can walk into a field where there are several flocks of sheep. When the shepherd speaks to them, the sheep that belong to that shepherd will separate from the other flocks and follow their shepherd. They can do this because they know their shepherd's voice. Likewise, if a shepherd from a different flock enters the field and calls to the sheep, the sheep that do not belong to his flock will move away from him. In our relationship with God, we need to recognize God's voice when He speaks to us. Likewise, we need to move far away from one who speaks and is not from God.

In Genesis, we read that the Lord walked in the Garden of Eden with Adam and Eve. There was no sin at that time, so God was able to meet face-to-face with His creation. After the fall of humankind,

God was no longer able to commune with His creation in the same manner due to sin. God still spoke to individuals, but He also gave revelation to prophets for His people. The prophets became the voice of God to those around them. In the New Testament, God gave some the gift of prophecy. This gift allows us to be the voice of God to other believers.

First Corinthians 14:1 tells us to desire spiritual gifts, especially prophecy. God emphasizes prophecy as the most desirable spiritual gift because it strengthens and helps the body of Christ to grow. The gift of prophecy is to strengthen, encourage, and comfort the body of Christ (1 Corinthians 14:3). It is a gift that brings the body of Christ closer to God.

A prophecy provides information about future events. A prophetic word can bring a revelation about something that is about to happen. However, it may also be about something that won't happen for many years. In 1 Samuel 9 and 10, we read a prophecy that a young man named Saul received. He was sent by his uncle to find some missing donkeys. He and a servant searched several different places over several days but could not find the missing donkeys. They were about to give up when the servant suggested they seek information from a nearby prophet. That inquiry turned into something much greater than a prophecy about a few donkeys. God used that opportunity to anoint Saul as king of Israel. At that time, Israel was petitioning God to appoint their first king. The first king would most likely come from one of the larger tribes on Israel. Saul becoming king was not likely, as Saul was from the tribe of Benjamin, which was the least of all of the tribes of Israel. However, the prophecy included a series of events that would take place that day. As Saul's day progressed, each event came to pass. Whatever doubt he had dissipated as he saw

God's word fulfilled. He could not deny that God had spoken to him through Samuel. History tells us that Saul became the first king of Israel in 1046 BC.

In Acts 27, Paul is on a ship on his way to stand trial in Rome. Along the journey, the ship had been experiencing rough weather. Paul warned his captors not to continue, or the ship and all of its cargo would be lost. Not heading Paul's warning, they continued toward Rome. After a few days of storms, the ship's workers threw all of the cargo overboard to lighten the ship's load in hopes that it would not sink. They continued to be battered by severe weather. The men on the ship became afraid that they would lose their lives to the storm. In Acts 27:23–26, Paul tells his captors that an angel appeared before him the previous night and assured him that no lives would be lost. After fourteen days, the ship hit a sandbar. They were near land, where they were able to swim to safety. No one died, just as Paul had prophesied.

God speaks to His people in a variety of ways. He gives us dreams and visions, speaks directly to us, or can give us an impression or sensation about a situation. We read in both the Old and New Testaments that God communicated to His people through visions and dreams (Joel 2:28–29; Numbers 12:6). God birthed the nation of Israel out of a vision given to Abraham (Genesis 15). In a vision, Peter saw a sheet full of various animals and reptiles coming from heaven. God told him to kill and eat the various animals. When Peter replied that he could not eat them because they were unclean, God spoke to him a second time. God used both a vision and His spoken word to talk to Peter (Acts 10:9–23), God spoke to Noah to build an ark (Genesis 6). Jesus could sense the thoughts of the Pharisees. "Immediately Jesus knew in his spirit that this was what they were thinking in their hearts, and he said to them, 'Why are you thinking these things?'" (Mark 2:8).

In Luke 1, we read three prophetic words. First, an angel appears to Zechariah in a vision and tells him that his wife, Elizabeth, is going to conceive a child in her old age. Second, an angel appears to Mary and tells her that she is going to conceive a son even though she is still a virgin. Third, the Holy Spirit filled Elizabeth, and she prophesied to Mary that she would give birth to the long-awaited Messiah. God uniquely spoke to each individual, just as He speaks to each of us through different means.

Prophecy can be for an individual, a group, or even a nation. In Genesis 46, God spoke to Jacob, assuring him of his family's safety in Egypt. He told him that He would multiply his family and then bring them back to the Promised Land. While this prophecy was for him as an individual, it also was for the nation of Israel. In our nation, presidents have sought the counsel of those who have the gift of prophecy.

While prophecy helps the believer to grow in their walk with God, it can also draw unbelievers to Christ. Paul wrote, "But if an unbeliever or an inquirer comes in while everyone is prophesying, they are convicted of sin and are brought under judgment by all, as the secrets of their hearts are laid bare. So they will fall down and worship God, exclaiming, 'God is really among you!'" (1 Corinthians 14:24–25).

When my husband was a teenager, he went to a dance at a mission in his hometown. At the time, he had not accepted Jesus Christ as his savior. He left the dance and wandered into another part of the mission where a prayer meeting was taking place. He stood at the back of the room, hoping not to be seen or recognized by anyone. One of the individuals at the prayer meeting began to prophesy. My husband knew the prophecy was for him. Because of that prophecy, my husband turned his life over to Christ.

A prophecy …

- speaks to future events
- can be about the immediate future or about events that won't take place for a season (1 Samuel 9–10, Acts 27)
- strengthens the body of Christ (1 Corinthians 14:3)
- encourages us as believers (1 Corinthians 14:3)
- can be for an individual, a group, or a nation (Genesis 46:1–4)
- brings unbelievers to Christ (1 Corinthians 14:24–25)

PROPHECY STUDY PAGES

Read Numbers 24:3–4.

What are the three ways that Balaam received prophecy?

1. _____
2. _____
3. _____

Read 1 Corinthians 14:1–5; 31–33.

Why does Paul tell the church at Corinth to eagerly desire spiritual gifts, especially prophecy (verse 4)?

_____

_____

What are the three benefits of prophecy listed in verse 3?

_____

_____

_____

What does Paul mean when he says, "The church may be edified" (verse 5)?

_____

_____

_____

_____

Who is in control of when a prophet speaks, and why is that important (verses 32–33)?

_____

_____

_____

_____

Read 2 Peter 1:19–21.

What does Peter mean when he says prophecy is "as to a light shining in a dark place" (verse 19)?

_____

_____

_____

_____

Where does prophecy originate, and who brings it to man (verse 21)?

_____

_____

_____

_____

Read Acts 2:17–18.

On whom does God pour out His spirit (verse 17)"

_____

_____

What happens to those who have God's spirit (verse 18)?

_____

_____

Ask the Lord to give you a word of prophecy for yourself or someone else. Write what He tells you here.

_____

_____

_____

_____

_____

_____

_____

_____

_____

_____

_____

_____

_____

_____

_____

_____

_____

WORD OF WISDOM

For this reason, since the day we heard about you, we have not stopped praying for you. We continually ask God to fill you with the knowledge of his will through all the wisdom and understanding that the Spirit gives.

—Colossians 1:9

T HERE ARE TWO kinds of wisdom. The first is humankind's wisdom. This is a natural, innate ability to view circumstances and make wise choices. We gain understanding of the world around us through experience and education. We can then apply our learned knowledge to make wise choices. However, God has a deeper and greater level of wisdom for His children. It is a wisdom given to us by God through the Holy Spirit, also known as a word of wisdom. God's wisdom fills us with "the knowledge of His will" for our lives (Colossians 1:9). It allows us to know the thoughts and purposes of God (Colossians 2:1–3).

Saul (later renamed Paul) was a tormentor to the early Christian church. The church was under attack. Christians were imprisoned and killed for their belief in Christ. In Saul's human understanding, he believed that the teachings of Jesus Christ were blasphemy. Saul went about the region torturing and killing Christians under the authority of the Roman government (Acts 8). After a dramatic conversion experience and being filled with the Holy Spirit, he began using the gift of wisdom and immediately began preaching the Gospel. He wrote a large portion of the New Testament through the God-given understanding he received.

Paul encouraged the believers in Corinth to allow the Holy Spirit to fill them. In doing so, they had access to understand the mysteries of God. Paul told the believers the world could not understand God's ways because they were only able to use human wisdom (1 Corinthians 2:1–16). In the same way, Paul began the letter to the believers in Colossae, encouraging them to allow the Spirit to fill them with divine wisdom so they could live a full life that was pleasing to God (Colossians 1:9–10).

Stephen was full of the Holy Spirit. God had given him the gifts of faith, miracles, and wisdom. When opposed by the Jewish leaders, God-given wisdom gave him the words to stand against his attackers. Even at the time of his death, Stephen continued to allow God's wisdom to provide him with the right words to say (Acts 6–7). Even as Stephen faced certain death, he turned to God and did not rely on his human understanding.

We receive words of wisdom by asking God. God generously gives us wisdom. He does not withhold from us. He gives to us without finding any fault in us for needing to ask (James 1:5). King Solomon asked God for wisdom. He found favor in God for asking. He could have asked for anything, but he chose wisdom. By doing so, God gave him far more than he requested. In 1 Kings 4:29, we read, "God gave Solomon wisdom and very great insight, and a breadth of understanding as measureless as the sand on the seashore." He was known as having greater wisdom than all other people on earth. Kings came from everywhere to have conversations with him and hear his God-given insight.

In 1 Kings 3:16–28, we read a story about two mothers who came to King Solomon for a decision. Both women claimed that the newborn baby belonged to them. They had both given birth to baby boys, but one of the babies had died. The mother of the dead baby switched the babies in the night. King Solomon used the wisdom of God to determine to whom the baby belonged. King Solomon relied on God to give him wisdom in this situation and many others.

When the Holy Spirit gives us the gift of wisdom, we lead a life that pleases God. As we grow in God's knowledge, we will have a desire to please God and make necessary changes. We will live a more fruitful life and be able to help others grow. It allows us to grow in God's knowledge, which shows in the way we conduct ourselves (Colossians 1:9–10).

Words of wisdom allow us to …

- know the thoughts and purposes of God (Colossians 2:1–3)
- know the mysteries of God (1 Corinthians 2:1–16)
- live a life that pleases God (Colossians 1:9–10)
- encourage other believers and bring unity to the body of Christ (Colossians 2:2–3)
- speak into the lives of leaders (Ephesians 3:10)
- face opposition (Acts 6)
- stand up against others who are relying on humankind's knowledge (1 Corinthians 2:11–16)

WORD OF WISDOM STUDY PAGES

Read Ephesians 3:1–13.

How was the mystery of God's grace made known to Paul (verse 3)"

_____

_____

Who does God want to use to reveal His wisdom (verse 10)?

_____

_____

How are we able to approach God with freedom and confidence (verse 12)?

Read 1 Corinthians 2. Describe God's wisdom.

_____

_____

What does God make known to us through wisdom and understanding (Ephesians 1:8–9)?

_____

_____

The spirit of wisdom and revelation allows us to _____ God better (Ephesians 1:17).

We can know God's _____ through wisdom and
spiritual understanding (Colossians 1:9).

If we lack wisdom, we are to ask God, and He will give it to us
_____ and without finding
_____(James 1:5).

What are the attributes of Godly wisdom listed in James 3:17?

_____	_____
_____	_____
_____	_____
_____	_____

Read 1 Kings 3:1–15 and 1 Kings 4:29–34.
What did Solomon ask of God?

_____

_____

What was God's response to Solomon's request?

_____

_____

Describe the wisdom given to Solomon.

_____

_____

WORD OF KNOWLEDGE

Before I formed you in the womb I knew you, before you were born I set you apart; I appointed you as a prophet to the nations.

—Jeremiah 1:5

GOD KNOWS US. He knows our thoughts and our desires. He has seen our past and our future. God is an intimate God. He knows how to reach us. A word of knowledge is a divine revelation given to believers by the Holy Spirit. This gift allows us to know information about a person or a situation that we would not otherwise know. God reveals Himself to another person by giving us a word of knowledge. A word of knowledge is a useful tool when ministering to others. The Holy Spirit shares the known to help people believe the unknown. The known opens a door for the Holy Spirit to speak to them undeniably.

Throughout scripture, we see God using words of knowledge for many different purposes. Jesus frequently had words of knowledge during His ministry on earth. Jesus used a word of knowledge to reveal Himself as the savior sent by God to unbelievers. On one occasion, he met a woman at a well in Samaria. Even though she was a stranger to Him, He spoke about her previous husbands and the man with whom she was currently living. He told her, "The fact is, you have had five husbands, and the man you now have is not your husband." She did not know how He knew this information. However, she recognized Him as being the Christ. This word of knowledge not only impacted her; it also impacted the community where she lived (John 4:5–30).

Often, Jesus spoke a word of knowledge to address the unbelief of the Pharisees. He knew their thoughts and countered their beliefs with the truth of who He was (Matthew 9:4; 22:15–22).

Jesus used a word of knowledge to remove doubt from those around Him. When Jesus requested Philip and Nathaniel to join him in ministry, Nathaniel had doubts that Jesus was the Messiah. Nathaniel asked, "How do you know me?" Jesus answered, "I saw you while you were still under the fig tree before Philip called you." Nathaniel believed that Jesus was the Christ because of a word of knowledge (John 1:43–51).

At the Last Supper, Jesus told the disciples that one of them would betray Him. He used a word of knowledge to remove any doubt that might try to come in during the three days He was in the grave. The disciples were able to believe the prophecies about the resurrection of Christ (John 13:18–30).

There was a season in my life where I was struggling. God sent a stranger to give me a prophetic word. As part of that word, she told me she saw me riding a bucking horse as a child. She didn't know I grew up riding horses. My dad would often bring horses to our house to train. I had ridden many bucking horses in my life. This picture she received of a bucking horse was a tiny part of the word she gave me, but it confirmed to me the rest of the prophetic word was from God.

After Jesus's death and resurrection, the Holy Spirit gave the disciples words of knowledge that allowed them to minister more effectively. In Acts 9, after Saul encountered God on the road to Damascus, he went to the house of Judas for three days. During that time, God gave Ananias a word of knowledge through a vision. Ananias was afraid because of Saul's reputation for torturing and killing Christians. However, Ananias was able to push past his fear and minister to Saul. The word of knowledge he received helped him know that God had changed Saul (Acts 9:1–19).

When I was ministering at my home church, the Lord gave me a word of knowledge. I was praying for a lady who was pregnant. I had not met her before and did not know her background. The Lord told me to pray for the baby she was carrying. He then gave me a word of knowledge that said, "This baby will not be like the last. This baby will live. It will not die." After we finished praying with her, she shared with me that she had recently given birth to a baby who died of a genetic disorder a few minutes after the birth. She was terrified that this baby might also die. When this baby was born, he also had a life-threatening genetic condition. She cried out to God and reminded Him of the word He gave her six months earlier. Despite ongoing health issues over the first year of his life, her baby continued to grow and gain strength. By the time he was a year old, the doctors told her that he was no longer in any danger. That baby is now a healthy young man. The mom was keenly aware that I had no information regarding the baby she had lost. The Holy Spirit used a word of knowledge to give her unshakeable faith to believe for her new baby's healing.

In the book of Joshua, we find the account of the Israelites taking the land that was promised to them, city by city. As they attempted to conquer the city of Ai, many Israelites lost their lives in the battle. Joshua went before the Lord to find out why they had been defeated. The Lord told him that there was sin in the camp. Joshua had the tribes of Israel report to him one by one. When the tribe of Judah stood before him, God revealed to him a word of knowledge. Achan, a soldier, had violated a covenant that Israel had with God. He stole items from a previous battle that the Lord specifically told Israel not to remove (Joshua 7).

We find a similar situation in the New Testament when the Lord revealed to Peter that Ananias and Saphira lied about the amount of money they received from the sale of their property (Acts 5:1–11). In both examples, God gave a word of knowledge to remove sin from His people.

In several accounts in the Old Testament, God gave a word of knowledge to a leader that allowed his people to defeat their enemies. One such time was when the Israelites were in a battle against Aram. God gave a word of knowledge to Israel, revealing where the Arameans were hiding. Because of this word of knowledge, they were able to trap their enemies and win the battle (2 Kings 6:8–12).

A word of knowledge …

- confirms the testimony of Christ to us (1 Corinthians 1:4–9)

- allows us to defeat our enemies (2 Kings 6:8–9; Matthew 22:15–22)
- cleanses sin from the church (Joshua 7:11–12; Acts 5:1–11)
- reveals God's work in us (Acts 9:1–19)
- drives out doubt (Matthew 9; John 1:43–51; John 13:19)
- allows us to push past our fears (Acts 9:1–19)

WORD OF KNOWLEDGE STUDY PAGES

Read Colossians 1.

Who gives us knowledge and understanding (verse 9)?

_____

_____

What are the benefits that come with knowledge from the Holy Spirit (verses 10–11)?

- We may live a life that is _____ of the Lord.
- We may _____ God.
- Bear _____ in every good work.
- Growing in the _____ of God.
- Strengthened with all _____ according to His glorious might.
- Have _____ and _____.

Read Acts 10.

What was the word of knowledge given to Cornelius (verse 6)?

_____

_____

How did Peter's vision and Cornelius's word of knowledge work together?

_____

_____

What happened to the group of people at Cornelius's house while Peter was speaking (verses 44–46)?

_____

_____

What was Peter's response to the Gentiles being filled with the Holy Spirit, and how did this event change his theology (verses 44–48)?

_____

_____

Do you have beliefs that changed when the Holy Spirit revealed something through a word of knowledge? If so, what were they, and how did they change?

_____

_____

GIFTS OF HEALING

Very truly I tell you, whoever believes in me will do the works
I have been doing, and they will do even greater things than
these, because I am going to the father.

—John 14:12

THE BIBLE IS full of examples of miraculous healings. In
each, there was a level of faith present. That faith was either
in the person needing the healing or the one praying for them. In
Matthew 9, we read examples of both. Jesus heals a paralyzed man
who is brought to Jesus by his friends. When Jesus saw the faith of
his friends, Jesus forgave the man's sins and healed him. In another
example, Jesus healed a woman who had a bleeding issue for twelve
years. He said to her, "Your faith has healed you." A blind man
approached Jesus and requested that Jesus heal his sight. Jesus said to
him, "According to your faith, let it be done to you." Later in the
same passage, Jesus removed those who lacked faith. Removing the
unbelief allowed Him to heal the daughter of the synagogue leader.
It was the faith of Jesus that not only healed her but raised her from
the dead.

Peter and John prayed for a man who had been lame his entire life. After the lame man got up and walked, the crowd was amazed. Peter addressed them and said, "By faith in the name of Jesus, this man whom you see and know was made strong. It is Jesus' name and the faith that comes through him that has completely healed him, as you can all see" (Acts 3:1–9). Peter talked about the faith that we have through Jesus. It was the faith that Peter and John possessed that allowed the man to receive healing.

We see later in Acts 14 that a lame man is healed. When Paul saw that the man had faith, he told the lame man to stand up. The man was able to walk for the first time in his life. Both Paul and the man who was healed had faith in God's healing power.

If we are going to move in the gift of healing, we must first have faith in God and His healing power. We must believe John 14:12 when it says we will do greater things than Christ did while He was on earth. We often see the gift of faith and the gift of healing working together in the same individual.

The gift of healing requires obedience. In 2 Kings 5, Naaman was suffering from leprosy. He went to a prophet, who instructed him to go to the River Jordan and dip seven times. At first, Naaman was offended. After a discussion with his servant, Naaman decided to obey, and he received his healing. If he had chosen to disobey, he would have continued to live with the debilitating disease.

A couple of years ago, I had been suffering from bursitis in my left shoulder for about six months. I was unable to raise my left arm or dress without assistance. If I tried to raise my arm, an excruciating pain would shoot through my shoulder. I had seen the doctor, but the condition continued to worsen. During the worship service at a women's conference, I heard God tell me to raise my hands to Him. At first, I hesitated to obey because I did not want to be in pain. I then realized that if God told me to lift my arm, He had a plan to heal me. I cautiously raised my hands into the air. The pain was gone. God miraculously healed me. To receive my healing, I had to obey God.

When moving in the gift of healing, God may tell us to do something unconventional. In the example given in John 9, Jesus made mud out of spit to heal a blind man. In 2 Kings 5, the prophet sent Naaman down to the River Jordan and told him to dip in the river seven times. In Acts 3, Peter instructed a lame man to get up and walk. God's ways do not always make sense to us. Our Western mindset teaches us to think logically. We look to science to explain things. Unfortunately, this mindset often robs us of the faith necessary to see miracles happen. God will ask us to do things that are outside our comfort zone. We must push through if we want to see the miraculous take place.

One night, a man came forward after our church service for prayer. When he walked up, God told my friend to put her fingers in the man's ears. She had a choice to either do what God told her to do or disobey. Faith allowed her to be obedient. When she placed her fingers in the man's ears, cancer cells began to fall to the ground. When she finished praying, the man told her that he had skin cancer on his ears and was scheduled for surgery to remove a good portion of his ear the following morning. He kept his appointment with the doctor, who declared him cancer-free.

God will use the gift of healing to further His kingdom and show Himself to unbelievers. In John 9, Jesus heals a man who had been blind since birth. When the disciples inquired about the reason for the man's blindness, Jesus said, "This happened so that the works of God might be displayed in him." After the blind man received healing, his friends and relatives recognized Jesus as Lord. Throughout the New Testament, we see many coming to Christ following miraculous healing. In Acts 2:14, we read, "More and more men and women believed in the Lord and were added to their number." During Jesus's ministry on earth, crowds gathered to hear what Jesus said because they saw someone they knew had miraculously healed. Jesus would use these times to address the onlookers and teach about God's love and salvation. In Matthew 4:23–25, we read, "Jesus went throughout Galilee, teaching in their synagogues, proclaiming the good news of the kingdom, and healing every disease and sickness among the people. News about him spread all over Syria, and people brought to him all who were ill with various diseases, those suffering severe pain, the demon-possessed, those having seizures, and the paralyzed; and he healed them. Large crowds from Galilee, the Decapolis, Jerusalem, Judea, and the region across the Jordan followed him."

The gift of healing …

- requires faith (Matthew 9)
- requires obedience (2 Kings 5)
- may require an unconventional action (Matthew 9; Acts 3)
- is a tool to reach unbelievers (Matthew 4)

GIFT OF HEALING STUDY PAGES

Read James 5:13–16.

What is the result of a prayer offered in faith (verse 15)?

_____

_____

What are the two characteristics of the "prayer of a righteous person" (verse 16)?

_____

_____

Read John 14:12–14.

What is the one who believes in Jesus able to do?

_____

_____

What did Jesus say would happen if we ask for something in His name?

_____

_____

Read Acts 3:1–10.

What did Peter say to the lame man (verse 6)?

_____

_____

When did the man's feet and ankles become strong (verse 7)?

_____

_____

Read Acts 4:1–21.

How many people accepted Christ as their savior after the lame man
was healed (Acts 4:4)?

_____

_____

How are Peter and John described in Acts 4:13?

_____

_____

Read Acts 5:12–16.

How did the people react to the signs and wonders?

_____

_____

What would happen today if people were being healed miraculously
in your town, state, or country?

_____

_____

What is the first step you could take to allow the Holy Spirit to use you in the area of healing?

_____

_____

Read 2 Timothy 1:5–7.
What does Paul tell Timothy to do in verse 6?

_____

_____

What does God's spirit give us (verse 7)?_____,

_____, and _____

WORKING OF MIRACLES

God also testified to it by signs, wonders, and various miracles
and by gifts of the Holy Spirit distributed according to his will.

—Hebrews 2:4

G OD IS THE miracle worker who created the universe, parted
the Red Sea, closed the mouths of lions, and raised Jesus from
the dead. The stories are endless of God's miracle-working power.
During Jesus's ministry on earth, He performed many miracles. The
disciples performed many miracles after Jesus returned to heaven.

A miracle is a supernatural event that cannot be done by a human.
It is a work that only God can do. We see that God uses miracles
as a sign to both believers and unbelievers. He establishes through
miracles that He is real and is God above all other gods.

If we follow the journey of the Israelites when God moved them
out of Egypt, we read that God used miracles to build a relationship
with the Israelites. The Israelites had been in Egypt for 430 years.
The Egyptians worshiped many different gods, and the Israelites
adopted many of these beliefs. While most of the Israelites practiced

Jewish customs, many of them did not believe in God. The Israelites moved to Egypt to take refuge from famine; however, their blessing had become their curse.

When God delivered the Israelites out of Egypt, there were two paths they could have taken. The first was a direct route from Egypt to the Promised Land. They could have traveled up the coastline. However, they would have immediately faced the Philistine army. God told Moses that if the Israelites took that route, many would return to Egypt (Exodus 13:17). Instead of taking the most direct course, God led them through the Sinai Desert, where they faced many obstacles. Throughout their journey, the Israelites experienced many miracles. God gave them direction using a cloud and fire (Exodus 13:21–22). He parted the Red Sea to allow them to escape their enemies (Exodus 14). He provided food and water daily as they crossed the desolate desert (Exodus 15–16). God told Moses that the Israelites would know that He was God by saving them from Pharaoh's army (Exodus 14:18, 31). He also told Moses the Israelites would know He was their God by the food He provided for them. Just as God used miracles to build a relationship with the Israelites as they journeyed from Egypt, He uses miracles today to build a relationship with us.

When I was in college, I had a car that would not go into reverse. I took the car to a mechanic, who said I needed a new transmission. At that time, I had just enough money to put gas in my car and buy my groceries. There was no money available for automotive repairs. I went back to my dorm room, discouraged and not sure how I was going to get to work the next day. I shared my situation with my friend Diana. She suggested we go lay hands on the car and pray for a miracle. We went down to the parking lot and laid hands on the hood of my car. After we prayed, I started the car and put it in reverse. It immediately went into gear and began to back up. I owned that car for another year and never had another issue with the transmission. God showed me His provision in my time of need. The moment God fixed the transmission in my car, I knew I had a relationship with a loving God that would always take care of my needs.

God also uses miracles to protect His children. God closed the mouths of the lions and saved Daniel from certain death (Daniel 6). God walked with Shadrach, Meshach, and Abednego while in the fiery furnace (Daniel 3). Balaam's donkey talked, which protected the Israelites from Balak (Numbers 22). We read many accounts of God protecting His people from harm.

One summer, I attended a school of ministry in Denver, Colorado, along with many other young men and women who were learning how to be more effective ministers. We had a day off to have some fun and decompress on July 4. Four of us rented a car and went exploring in the beautiful mountains. On the way back to the campus, we encountered a great deal of traffic. There were multiple lanes of traffic moving in both directions at high speeds. The person in the car to our right decided to change lanes suddenly. Our car was in his blind spot, and he did not see us. When he changed lanes, his vehicle came over the top of the hood of our car. The front of our car became fluid and absorbed the other car. Both vehicles were occupying the same space for a few seconds. I slowed our car to allow room for him to pull ahead. His car separated from the front of our car, and our car became solid once again. I pulled over at the next off-ramp and inspected the car for damage. There was none. All four of us were shaken but elated, as we had all seen the same thing. God had done a miracle, and we were unharmed. We sat in the parking lot for several minutes, discussing what had just happened. We knew we had experienced a miracle. God had protected us from what would have been a severe accident that day.

God uses miracles to show Himself to unbelievers. One of my favorite Bible stories as a child was when the prophets of Baal and Elijah faced off. The people of Israel came around two altars. One altar was built to honor Baal (a false god), and one was created to honor God. Four hundred and fifty prophets of Baal gathered, placed a meat sacrifice upon the altar, and began praying to Baal. After many hours of begging Baal to bring down fire to consume their sacrifice, nothing happened. Elijah then placed his sacrifice on the altar and poured twelve massive jugs of water over the sacrifice. There was so much water that it not only covered the sacrifice and the altar, but it also filled the moat around the altar. Elijah then prayed to God. God sent down a fire that consumed the offering, wood, stones of the altar, and all of the water. God performed a miracle as a sign to the people who were unbelievers. The people turned back to God after they had experienced his miraculous power (1 Kings 18:16–39).

In the world today, people worship many different gods. They are looking for miracles. When we turn on the television, many shows have "miracles" as part of their plot. However, they are directing people toward false gods. Like the people of Israel in 1 Kings, they are being led astray by false gods. If we are to see true revival in our times, it is going to require the church body to move in the gift of miracles. People need to see a powerful God.

Like the other gifts, the gift of miracles requires faith. We must believe God is all-powerful and will fulfill His word. If God speaks to us and tells us to pray for a miracle, we must have faith to believe that God will do the miracle that He promised. Take a moment and imagine a world where God's power was unleashed and miracles were taking place. Think about the impact that would have on those around us.

God uses miracles to …

- show Himself to his people
- protect His children
- lead unbelievers into salvation

WORKING OF MIRACLES STUDY PAGES

Read John 2:1–12.

After Jesus turns the water into wine, what is the response of the disciples?

_____

_____

What did this miracle reveal (verse 11)?

_____

_____

Read Matthew 14:13–34.

What was the response of the disciples when Jesus gave them instructions (verse 18–20)?

_____

_____

Why did Jesus go off by himself (verse 23)?

_____

_____

When Peter recognized Jesus, he was full of faith. Why do you think his faith faltered (verse 30–31)?

_____

_____

How do we keep our faith from faltering?

_____

_____

What was the response of the people of Gennesaret when Jesus came to their city (verses 34–36)?

_____

_____

If you move in the gift of miracles, how do you think people in your community might respond?

_____

_____

Read Matthew 15:29–31.
What was the response of the crowd when Jesus performed miracles (verse 31)?

_____

_____

Read Matthew 16:5–14.
Why did Jesus warn the disciples about the Pharisees and Sadducees (verse 13)?

_____

_____

Who are the Pharisees and Sadducees today? How do we guard against them?

_____

_____

DISCERNING OF SPIRITS

For our struggle is not against flesh and blood, but against the rulers, against the authorities, against the powers of this dark world and against the spiritual forces of evil in the heavenly realms.

—Ephesians 6:12 (NIV)

WE ARE IN a battle! There is no denying it. If you have been a Christian long, you have faced opposition. Satan would love nothing more than to discourage you or, better yet, make you bitter toward God. Discerning of spirits gives us the ability to see into the spirit world. It allows us to judge if a spirit is from God or is evil. Satan masquerades as an angel of light (2 Corinthians 11:14). He is the father of lies (John 8:44). His highest goal is to kill, steal, and destroy Christians (John 10:10). Satan lies. He tries to convince us that his plans are from God. In 2 Corinthians 11:14, we are told Satan masquerades as an angel of light. However, God has given us weapons to stand against our enemy. God gives us discernment so we can reveal the enemy's plans.

There are angels as well as demons that are at work. In Numbers 22, we read the story of Balaam. Balak, the king of Moab, summoned Balaam to curse the Israelites. Balaam was a diviner. The Israelites had camped outside Moab, and Balak feared an attack. When Balaam set out to go to Balak, his donkey saw an angel of the Lord standing in the road. The donkey refused to go forward and went into a field. Each time Balaam tried to get the donkey to go in a different direction, it refused. Balaam became angry with the donkey. In verse 31, we read, "God opened Balaam's eyes, and he saw an angel of the Lord." God gave Balaam discernment. He realized it was God who was opposing him.

In 2 Kings 6, Elisha was surrounded by an enemy army, but he was not afraid. When his servant began to worry and question what to do, Elisha prayed that God would give his servant discernment by opening his eyes into the spirit world. The servant was able to see God's army surrounding them. By seeing into the spiritual realm, he knew God was protecting them.

We adopted my daughter April when she was four years old. At first, she acted out, in hopes of being sent back to her birth mother. One morning, she came to me and told me she had seen an angel. The angel told her of God's plan for us to be her parents. Her attitude toward us changed with that encounter. God had opened her eyes.

Likewise, discerning of spirits helps us fight against Satan's evil plans. In 1 Peter 5:8, we are told the devil roams like a lion, wishing to destroy Christians. We need to be aware of his plans if we are to defeat him. God has gifted His church with the ability to know the schemes of the devil so that we will not become trapped by the devil's plans (1 Timothy 3:7).

In Matthew 4, about Jesus fasting in the desert. He had been brought there by a spirit sent from God, but the devil came to tempt him. Jesus was able to discern the spirit was not from God and resist his attempts to destroy His ministry before it had even begun.

During Christ's ministry on earth, He delivered many from demons. When Jesus was visiting Peter's house, people who were possessed by demons came to Jesus (Matthew 8). When Jesus sent the disciples out to begin ministering without Him, he told them, "Heal the sick, raise the dead, cleanse those who have leprosy, drive out demons. Freely you have received; freely give" (Matthew 10:8 NIV).

Paul and Silas were ministering together when a fortune-teller began following them around and shouting. She continued disrupting their ministry for several days. Paul finally turned to her and told the demon that possessed her to get out. The demon left her (Acts 16:16–18). Paul was able to discern that the spirit that allowed her to speak of future events was not of God.

The spirit world is genuine. Angels are fighting on our behalf. Satan has his minions working to keep us from growing closer to God. At church one Sunday, I saw angels all around, praising God with us during the worship service. One of the angels went over to a young mom in our congregation. The angel poured a vile of healing oil over her head. As the oil ran down her head, she began to cry. God was healing her heart from the hurts of her past. After church, I went to her and told her the vision God had shown me. She said that during the worship service, she knew God had touched her. She confirmed that there were many past hurts she had been asking God to heal. God allowed me to see into the spirit world to reinforce to her what God was doing in her heart.

In Daniel 10, we read that an angel appeared to Daniel. The angel was delayed for three weeks because he was in a battle with a demon assigned to the kingdom of Persia. The battles fought on our behalf are very real. Likewise, the actions set out to destroy us as believers are equally as real. There is a spirit world that can only be discerned by the Holy Spirit in us. The gift of discerning of spirits is necessary if the church is going to stand against the enemy of our souls effectively.

Discerning of spirits ...

- allows us to see into the spirit world
- protects us from Satan's plans to destroy us
- uncovers the lies of the enemy
- opens our eyes to angels
- shows us God is at work in our lives

DISCERNING OF SPIRITS STUDY PAGES

Read Acts 7:54–60.

How did Stephen's ability to discern the spirit world help him at the time of his death?

_____

_____

Read Acts 8:26–40.

What was the outcome of Philip's encounter with an angel?

_____

_____

Read Ephesians 6:10–12.

Who is our enemy in verse 12?

_____

_____

How does knowing Satan's plans help you to defeat him?

_____

_____

Read 1 John 4:1–6.

What are we told to do to the spirits in verse 1?

_____

_____

We are to test the spirits against God's Word. How do we know if a message is not from God?

_____

_____

Read 2 Corinthians 11:12–15.

What does it mean to masquerade?

_____

_____

How can we see past the disguise?

_____

_____

Read Revelation 1:1–3.

Who appeared to John (verse 1)?

_____

_____

What did John do with the vision revealed to him (verse 2)?

_____

_____

What benefit do we receive from John's encounter with the angel (verse 3)?

_____

_____

When we encounter the spirits sent from God, how can we impact those around us?

_____

_____

TONGUES AND INTERPRETATION

> When the day of Pentecost came, they were all together in one place. Suddenly a sound like the blowing of a violent wind came from heaven and filled the whole house where they were sitting. They saw what seemed to be tongues of fire that separated and came to rest on each of them. All of them were filled with the Holy Spirit and began to speak in other tongues as the Spirit enabled them.
>
> —Acts 2:1–4

THE GIFT OF tongues is the ability to speak in a foreign language you have never learned. Acts 2 is the first reference in scripture to the gift of tongues. Jesus had ascended into heaven. The disciples and several other believers (about 120 in all) were in Jerusalem, praying together. It was the day of Pentecost, which was the celebration of the wheat harvest (Exodus 34:22; Leviticus 23:15–22). The town of Jerusalem was full of people from all over the world celebrating. The Holy Spirit filled the believers, and they began to preach about Jesus in foreign languages. A crowd gathered, and Peter stood up with the other disciples and preached of Jesus's resurrection. About three thousand people got saved that day.

In Acts 19, Paul is in Ephesus. He is speaking to several believers. The believers had been baptized in water but had not yet received the gifts of the spirit. Paul laid hands on them, and they began speaking with the gift of tongues.

When Paul wrote the first book of Corinthians, he discussed the purposes of tongues. When we speak in tongues, we speak to God (1 Corinthians 14:2). By speaking in tongues to God, we edify or build ourselves up. Paul tells us that when we speak in tongues, we pray with our spirit (1Corinthians 14:14–15). Additionally, speaking in tongues is also a sign for unbelievers, as we saw in Acts 2.

There are two prophecies about tongues. In Isaiah 28:11. we read, "Very well then, with foreign lips and strange tongues God will speak to this people." In Mark, we read that Jesus had risen from the dead and was speaking with His disciples. He told them, "And these signs will accompany those who believe: In my name, they will drive out demons; they will speak in new tongues" (Mark 16:17).

I included the gifts of tongues and interpretation together in this chapter, as it is difficult to separate them. They operate together. The gift of interpretation is the supernatural ability to understand what is being said when someone speaks with the gift of tongues. There are only two references in scripture to the interpretation of tongues. In Acts 12, Paul lists interpretation as one of the gifts of the Spirit. In 1 Corinthians 14, Paul cautions the church in Corinth that if they are going to speak in tongues during the church service, there needs to be an interpretation; otherwise, it doesn't benefit anyone except the person speaking.

Tongues …

- is a sign for unbelievers
- is speaking to God in the spirit
- edifies us
- should be interpreted if spoken in church

Interpretation …

- allows the church to benefit from the gift of tongues

TONGUES AND INTERPRETATION STUDY PAGES

Read Mark 16:15–18.

What are the signs that will follow those who believe?

_____

_____

Read Acts 2:1–12 and Deuteronomy 26:1–10.
Why were so many people in Jerusalem on the day of Pentecost?
What were they celebrating?

_____

_____

Why do you think God chose the Feast of Harvest (Pentecost) to reveal the Holy Spirit to His disciples?

_____

_____

What enabled them to speak in tongues that they had never learned (verse 4)?

_____

_____

What was the reaction of the crowd when they heard Galileans speaking in foreign languages (verses 6–12)?

_____

_____

Read 1 Corinthians 14:1–5.
Who are you speaking to when you speak in tongues (verse 2)?

_____

_____

Who is edified when you speak in tongues (verse 4)?

_____

_____

How is the church edified when someone speaks in tongues (verse 5)?

_____

_____

Read 1 Corinthians 14:13–17.
In the church setting, if you speak in tongues, what are you to do?

_____

_____

What part of you is praying when you are praying in tongues (verse 14)?

_____

_____

ACTIVATING THE GIFTS

"For this reason, I remind you to fan into flame the gift of God, which is in you through the laying on of my hands."

—2 Timothy 1:6

I N ACTS 1, Luke recounts Jesus's last minutes on earth. He was with the disciples and told them they would receive the baptism of the Holy Spirit. It was the gift Jesus was leaving for them (and us) when He returned to heaven. He explained that with this baptism of the Holy Spirit, they would receive a power that would allow them to spread His message of salvation to all nations.

In Acts 19, Paul traveled to Ephesus. He asked the believers there if they had received the Holy Spirit. They had not yet received the baptism of the Holy Spirit. When Paul laid his hands on them, they were filled with the Holy Spirit and began speaking in tongues and prophesying. We receive the gifts of the spirit through the laying on of hands (2 Timothy 1:6). There is an impartation of the Spirit that takes place when we lay hands on one another and pray.

In Acts 2, Peter is preaching to a crowd of people. He tells them to repent, be baptized, and receive the Holy Spirit. The gifts are for *all* believers, not just a select few. They give us the power to reach the lost. They allow us to build one another up in the church. They help us to reach the lost.

We are to stir up the gifts. As believers, we can begin to seek the gifts and move in faith, knowing that God is faithful to fulfill his word. Here are some practical ways to begin. In 1994, I began attending a new church. On Wednesday nights, they had the school of ministry. On these nights, the pastor would teach a short lesson on one of the gifts, and then we would practice moving in those gifts. At first, I was apprehensive. I soon learned that they were stirring up the gifts as scripture instructs. We were putting action to our faith. Below are some of the exercises or activations we would do that got us moving in the gifts at a deeper level.

Before beginning any of the activations below, pray as a group for a couple of minutes. Allow time for each person to focus on God. Have them confess their sins, give their burdens to God, and allow the Holy Spirit to fill them with His presence. If this is a group that is just learning and beginning to move in the gifts of the spirit, have them give one another permission to practice hearing from God. It has been my experience that God always shows up, but we don't want those who are just learning to feel that they must be perfect. That would prevent them from hearing from God.

- If someone in your group has never been filled with the baptism of the Holy Spirit, lay hands on them and pray. Have them speak out any sounds they hear or are sensing. It may sound like nonsense at first, but they will soon realize that God is at work.

- Ask God to give you a prophetic word for yourself. Write down whatever you hear, see, or sense. Try not to filter what you write, but write it as quickly as it comes to you. It doesn't have to be profound or complicated. Trust that God wants to speak to you.

- Get together with another believer who wants to move in the gifts as well. Pray for each other. Ask God to show you something for the other person. Tell them what you hear, see, or sense. Give each other permission to learn. One time, our small group was doing this activation. One of the people got a simple picture that she thought didn't have any meaning. She said she saw a house on a tree-covered hill. In front of the house was a For Sale sign. The lady the word was for had been seeking God about selling her home. Her house sat on top of a hill covered in almond trees. This simple word confirmed what she had been sensing. God can use even simple pictures to impact others.

- In a small group, give each person a piece of paper and have them write their name on the back. Collect the papers and randomly distribute them to the group. Without looking at the name on the back, ask God to give each person a word for the one the piece of paper belongs to. Have them write down whatever they hear, see, or sense.

- In a larger group, number off into two even groups. Have one group form a circle facing out and the other group form a circle facing the inner circle. Each person should have a partner. Have each person seek God for a word for their partner. Once both people have had an opportunity to share what the Lord has given them, rotate the outer circle clockwise. Everyone should have a new partner. Repeat several times until each person has prophesied to multiple people.

- In a group, have anyone who is sick or has an injury come to the middle of the group. Gather around and pray for healing. Believe God for miraculous healing. Ask the individuals to share any changes they are sensing in their bodies.

- In groups of four to five people, have one person get in the middle, and the others circle that person. Have the person in the middle ask God for a word of prophecy, knowledge, or wisdom for each person in the circle.

Be creative and find ways to stir up the gifts in yourself and those with whom you are ministering. Allow faith to grow through this process. As you begin to put action with your faith in God, you will see God do amazing things.

GIFTS OF THE SPIRIT ANSWER KEY

Read Acts 1. What were the disciples doing before being filled with the Holy Spirit?

They were waiting in Jerusalem and praying for the gift that Jesus had promised them.

According to 2 Chronicles 8:12–13, what were the three annual festivals celebrated by the Israelites?

Festival of Unleavened Bread

Festival of Weeks

Festival of Tabernacles

Which of these three festivals were the people celebrating in Acts 1–2? **Festival of Weeks.**

Read Exodus 34:22–27. The Celebration of Weeks was part of a covenant God made with Israel. Write down everything God promised to do as His part of the covenant.

Drive out our enemies and enlarge our territories.

What does it mean to you to have your territories enlarged? **(Answers will vary.)**

In Luke 24:49, Jesus told the disciples he would clothe them in **power** from on **High**.

Read Mark 16:15–18. What signs does Jesus say will accompany believers? **Drive out demons; speak in new tongues; pick up snakes unharmed; drink poison unharmed; heal the sick.**

After the disciples received the Holy Spirit in Acts 2, Peter stood up and addressed the crowd. Read Acts 2:14–41. Who did Peter say this promise is for (verse 39)? **You, your children, all who are far off, and all whom the Lord our God will call.**

Peter quotes Joel 2:28–32. To whom will God pour out His spirit? **All people.**

In Acts 2:22, Peter states that God accredited Jesus by **miracles, wonders,** and **signs.**

As we continue to study each gift individually, ask God to open your heart and mind to receive all that He has for you. Use the space below to write a commitment to God to open yourself up to fresh revelations. **(Answers will vary.)**

FAITH ANSWER KEY

Read Genesis 15:1–6.

What is credited as righteousness? **Abraham believed the Lord (faith)**.

Read 1 Corinthians 2.

What produces faith (verse 5)? **God's power.**

How does having the Holy Spirit help us to have faith (verse 11–12)? **The Holy Spirit knows the thoughts of God. The Holy Spirit teaches us the ways and thoughts of God. Knowing God's thoughts produces faith.**

Look at each person listed in Hebrews 11. What were they able to do because of their faith in God?

Brought God a better offering; left earth without dying; built an ark; received an inheritance; had children in old age; birthed a nation; passed God's test; blessed his children; prophesied the release of the Israelites from Egypt; shielded their child from death; gave up luxury to serve God; led the Israelites out of Egypt; kept the Passover and prevented death

from killing his family; passed through the Red Sea on dry land; won the battle of Jericho; hid spies and avoided death.

In Mark 16:15–20, who does Jesus say will cast out demons, speak in tongues, pick up snakes and drink poison safely, and heal the sick? **Those who believe.**

Read Luke 24:46–49 and Acts 1:4–6.

Jesus tells the disciples to wait in the city for the Holy Spirit. What does He say they will be clothed with when they receive the Holy Spirit? **Power from on High.**

Read James 2:14–25.

What needs to accompany faith for it to be fruitful? **Action.**

How do faith and action work together? **Faith and action work together; faith is made complete with action.**

What happens to faith without action? **Dead or useless.**

Read Ephesians 6:16. How does faith shield us? **It protects us from anything the enemy throws at us.**

What does faith do to our enemies? **Extinguishes his arrows or his attacks.**

What are some ways you can stir up the gift of faith in your own life? How will that help you to move in the other gifts of the spirit? **(Answers will vary.)**

PROPHECY ANSWER KEY

Read Numbers 24:3–4.

What are the three ways that Balaam received prophecy?

Saw with his eyes.
Heard God's words.
Had a vision.

Read 1 Corinthians 14:1–5; 31–33.

Why does Paul tell the church at Corinth to eagerly desire spiritual gifts, especially prophecy (verse 4)? **Prophesy edifies the church.**

What are the three benefits of prophecy listed in verse 3? **Prophecy strengthens, encourages, and comforts the people who hear it.**

What does Paul mean when he says, "The church may be edified" (verse 5)? **It will benefit spiritually.**

Who is in control of when a prophet speaks, and why is that important (verse 32–33)? **The prophet is in control of their body. The use**

of gifts in a church service should be done in an orderly manner.

Read 2 Peter 1:19–21.

What does Peter mean when he says prophecy is "as to a light shining in a dark place" (verse 19)? **(Answers will vary but should include something like "Prophecy sheds light on God's plans.")**

Where does prophecy originate, and who brings it to humans (verse 21)? **All prophecy comes from God and is given to humans by the Holy Spirit.**

Read Acts 2:17–18.

On whom does God pour out His spirit (verse 17)? **All people.**

What happens to those who have God's spirit (verse 18)? **They will prophesy.**

Ask the Lord to give you a word of prophecy for yourself or someone else. Write what He tells you here. **(Answers will vary.)**

WORD OF WISDOM ANSWER KEY

Read Ephesians 3:1–13.

How was the mystery of God's grace made known to Paul (verse 3)?
Through revelation from God.

Who does God want to use to reveal His wisdom (verse 10)? **The church.**

How are we able to approach God with freedom and confidence (verse 12)? **Through faith in God.**

Read 1 Corinthians 2. Describe God's wisdom. **God's wisdom is revealed to us by the Holy Spirit. The Holy Spirit knows God's thoughts and reveals spiritual truths to us. God's wisdom gives us the mind of Christ.**

What does God make known to us through wisdom and understanding (Ephesians 1:8–9)? **The mysteries of God's will.**

The spirit of wisdom and revelation allows us to **know** God better (Ephesians 1:17).

We can know God's **will**   through wisdom and spiritual understanding (Colossians 1:9).

If we lack wisdom, we are to ask God, and He will give it to us **generously** and without finding **fault** (James 1:5).

What are the attributes of Godly wisdom listed in James 3:17?

pure	**full of mercy**
peace-loving	**good fruit**
considerate	**impartial**
submissive	**sincere**

Read 1 Kings 3:1–15 and 1 Kings 4:29–34.

What did Solomon ask of God? **A discerning heart; wisdom.**

What was God's response to Solomon's request? **God was pleased and blessed Solomon.**

Describe the wisdom given to Solomon. **Measureless, greater than anyone in the world.**

WORD OF KNOWLEDGE ANSWER KEY

Read Colossians 1.

Who gives us knowledge and understanding (verse 9)? **God.**

What are the benefits that come with the gift of knowledge from the Holy Spirit (verse 10–11)?

- We may live a life that is **worthy** of the Lord.
- We may **please** God.
- Bear **fruit** in every good work.
- Growing in the **knowledge** of God.
- Strengthened with all **power** according to His glorious might.
- Have great **endurance** and **patience.**

Read Acts 10.

What was the word of knowledge given to Cornelius (verse 6)? **Peter was staying in Simon's house.**

How did Peter's vision and Cornelius's word of knowledge work together? **Peter's vision showed him that it was OK to go to**

Cornelius even though Cornelius was a Gentile and Peter was a Jew.

What happened to the group of people at Cornelius's house while Peter was speaking (verse 44–46)? **They received the Holy Spirit, speaking in tongues and praising God.**

What was Peter's response to the Gentiles being filled with the Holy Spirit, and how did this event change his theology (verse 44–48)? **He was astonished but recognized that God wanted them to be baptized just as the Jews had been baptized.**

Do you have beliefs that the Holy Spirit has changed through a word of knowledge? If so, what were they and how did they change? **(Answers will vary.)**

GIFT OF HEALING ANSWER KEY

Read James 5:13–16.

What is the result of a prayer offered in faith (verse 15)? **The sick will be healed and forgiven.**

What are the two characteristics of the "prayer of a righteous person" (verse 16)? **Powerful**

and **effective.**

Read John 14:12–14.

What is the one who believes in Jesus able to do? **They will do the things Jesus did and even more.**

What did Jesus say would happen if we ask for something in His name? **It will be done.**

Read Acts 3:1–10.

What did Peter say to the lame man (verse 6)? **He commanded him to walk.**

When did the man's feet and ankles become strong (verse 7)? **Once he stood up.**

How many people accepted Christ as their savior when the lame man was healed (Acts 4:4)? **About five thousand.**

How are Peter and John described in Acts 4:13? **Unschooled** and **ordinary.**

Read Acts 5:12–16.

How did the people react to the signs and wonders? **They brought the sick and tormented to be healed.**

What would happen today if people were being healed miraculously in your town, state, or country? **(Answers will vary.)** What is the first step you could take to allow the Holy Spirit to use you in the area of healing? **(Answers will vary.)**

Read 2 Timothy 1:5–7.

What does Paul tell Timothy to do in verse 6? **Fan into flame the gift of God.**

What does God's spirit give us (verse 7)? **Power** , **love** , and **self-discipline.**

WORKING OF MIRACLES ANSWER KEY

Read John 2:1–12.

After Jesus turns the water into wine, what is the response of the disciples (verse 11)? **They believed in him.**

What did this miracle reveal (verse 11)? **It revealed God's glory present in Jesus.**

Read Matthew 14:13–34.

What was the response of the disciples when Jesus gave them instructions (verse 18–20)? **They did what Jesus said to do.**

Why did Jesus go off by Himself (verse 23)? **He went to pray.**

When Peter recognized Jesus, He was full of faith. Why do you think his faith faltered (30–31)? **He allowed fear to be greater than his faith.**

How do we keep our faith from faltering? **(Answers will vary.)**

What was the response of the people of Gennesaret when Jesus came to their city (verse 34–36)? **They sent word to their friends and**

family of His presence. They brought the sick to Him to be healed.

If you move in the gift of miracles, how do you think people in your community might respond?

(Answers will vary.)

Read Matthew 15:29–31.

What was the response of the crowd when Jesus performed miracles (verse 31)? **They were amazed, and they praised God.**

Read Matthew 16:5–14.

Why did Jesus warn the disciples about the Pharisees and Sadducees (verse 12)?

They were to guard against the false teachings of the Pharisees and Sadducees.

Who are the Pharisees and Sadducees today? How do we guard against them? **(Answers will vary.)**

DISCERNING OF SPIRITS ANSWER KEY

Read Acts 7:54–60.

How did Stephen's ability to discern the spirit world help him at the time of his death?

(Answers will vary.)

Read Acts 8:26–40.

What was the outcome of Philip's encounter with an angel? **The Ethiopian was saved and baptized.**

Read Ephesians 6:10–12.

Who is our enemy (verse 12)? **The devil**

How does knowing Satan's plans help you to defeat him? **(Answers will vary.)**

Read 1 John 4:1–6.

What are we told to do to the spirits in verse 1? **Test them to see whether they are from God.**

We are to test the spirits against God's Word. How do we know if a message is not from God? **It will not line up with God's Word.**

Read 2 Corinthians 11:12–15.

What does it mean to masquerade? **Disguise oneself or pretend to be something that you are not.**

How can we see past the disguise? **We need discernment that comes from the Holy Spirit.**

Read Revelation 1:1–3.

Who appeared to John (verse 1)? **An angel.**

What did John do with the vision revealed to him (verse 2)? **He testified to it, or he wrote it down.**

What benefit do we receive from John's encounter with the angel (verse 3)? **We are blessed when we read it aloud.**

When we encounter the spirits sent from God, how can we impact those around us? **(Answers will vary.)**

TONGUES AND INTERPRETATION ANSWER KEY

Read Mark 16:15–18.

What are the signs that will follow those who believe? **Drive out demons, speak in tongues, pick up snakes and eat poison without being harmed, heal the sick.**

Read Acts 2:1–12 and Deuteronomy 26:1–10.

Why were so many people in Jerusalem on the day of Pentecost? What were they celebrating? **They were there for the Feast of Weeks, which is the celebration of the wheat harvest.**

Why do you think God chose the Feast of Harvest (Pentecost) to reveal the Holy Spirit to His disciples?

(Answers will vary.)

What enabled them to speak in tongues that they had never learned (verse 4)? **The Holy Spirit enabled them.**

What was the reaction of the crowd when they heard Galileans speaking in foreign languages (verse 6–12)? **They were bewildered, amazed, and perplexed, and they made fun of them.**

Read 1 Corinthians 14:1–5.

Who are you speaking to when you speak in tongues (verse 2)? **God.**

Who is edified when you speak in tongues (verse 4)? **The one who is speaking.**

How is the church edified when someone speaks in tongues (verse 5)? **When there is an interpreter.**

Read 1 Corinthians 14:13–17.

In the church setting, if you speak in tongues, what are you to do (verse 13)? **Pray that someone will interpret what you say.**

What part of you is praying when you are praying in tongues (verse 14)? **Your spirit.**

Printed in the United States
by Baker & Taylor Publisher Services